WISDOM FEAST

Wahida Mohamed

Wisdom Feast Ltd
London

Published 2021 by Wisdom Feast Ltd Studio
210 Curtain House, 134-146 Curtain Road, London EC2A 3AR

ISBN: 978-1-73995-580-9 (print)
ISBN: 978-1-73995-581-6 (eBook)

What would you like to be remembered for?

A jewelry box full of inspirational stories for a happy, fulfilled life. Great memories for a wonderful life.

Introduction

On a Thursday afternoon, I decided to go for a walk in Elm Park, just to unwind and clear my head before going back to the school where I was teaching. As I started my healthy walk, I could see an old woman sitting on a bench, one I knew too well, as this message was written on it: "to my beloved wife, Katharine Campbell, who loved spending her afternoons in this peaceful park."

The ancestral trees were standing: tall, verdant, and mature, some were dark and most severe, while others were younger, thicker, and healthy. This woman was one with nature. It was somehow comforting watching her. As I approached the bench, I was animated by curiosity. *Who was she? Why was she sitting there alone?* Her face was candid, her grey hair reflected the sunlight, her face seemed to be marked by a very long life filled with ups and downs. She was watching people passing by, until our eyes met. She gave me a beautiful smile, a smile I returned immediately and naturally, as I felt a connection. At that moment, I wanted to sit next to her and ask her questions about her life. I wanted to know her story. But I was short on time and had to be back to school.

As I walked back to school, I reflected on this. "What wisdom does this woman have to share from the many decades she has lived and that I would benefit from?"

I would love to have had the time to talk with her, listen to her story and learn the wisdom that she has for all of us. I vowed in that moment that someday, I would capture stories of others and make them available for sharing.

As a teacher, I know that stories are the best way to convey life lessons. Human beings and their emotions, and life experiences were analyzed in class, leading to understanding, and encouraging self-introspection. Discovering those stories, I believe, will have a positive impact in the future lives of teenagers and young adults and will be a motor to their personal growth, a priceless tool to educate our future generation. Each story is one that conveys a life lesson.

- You will have stories you can read to your children on a whole range of life lessons.
- You will be inspired to listen to the stories of the elders in your own family and the wisdom they can impart.
- Ultimately, you will have an impact on the young people in your life because they will listen to a life lesson in the most compelling way possible, as a part of a story.

"Giving a voice to the wise ones, mature adults who have a story to tell, their story."

—WAHIDA MOHAMED

"Expanding our minds and harness new possibilities. Engaging in stimulating discussions."

—WAHIDA MOHAMED

If you would like to share your story and leave behind a generous life testament that will benefit future generations, join Wahida on her weekly podcast: "My success, my story." Send your request via the website or send a direct email.

www.wahidamohamed.com
wahida@wahidamohamed.com

Contents

Introduction vii

Acknowledgments 1

One
The Miracle of Life: "Remember to Breathe Some Fresh Air" 2

Two
Imagine, You Create: "Have a Go at It, You Are More Able than You Think" 4

Three
Growing Up: "Know Who You Are, It Does Not Matter Where You Come From" 6

Four
Run and Score: "Look after Yourself, Really Nurture Yourself and Your Wants." 10

Five
My First Trip: "Keep Your Dreams Alive, Don't Lose Track of Them" 13

Six
My Wedding: "Collect Many Memories of Your Childhood, They Are Priceless" 17

Seven
The Land of Hopes: "Be Free to Be Who You Want to Be" 21

Eight
My Regrowth: "Drink in Moderation, Don't Deny if You Have a Problem" 24

Nine
Changes: "Believe in Yourself! Go and Venture the World" 28

Ten
A New Dawn, a New Me: "Stop and Rewind, Take the Time to Find Yourself" 32

Eleven
A Love Reality: "Never Give up on Your Aspirations, Your Desires!" 36

Twelve
A Recipe for Happiness: "Slow the Heartbeat, Breathe, Enjoy Each Moment" 39

Thirteen
Healthy Life: "Keep Yourself Active" 41

Fourteen
Fond Memories: "Embrace Life, Make the Most of It" 44

Conclusion 47

About the Author 49

Acknowledgments

I would like to express my love and gratitude to the following people.

My husband, Thomas, for his support and understanding as I spent many nights writing, creating my very first book that you are now holding in your precious hands, and I hope will be shared with many of your loved ones for many years to come.

My parents, who have been a great source of inspiration. I grew up listening to many of their stories, and this is where my love of storytelling comes from.

My sisters, we have shared so many great memories together. Chrysoula C., Veronica K., Pamela M., Pat P., Dagmar H., and Brenda S., for either sharing their own stories or stories recounted by loved ones. They have been encouraged to share many details of their personal lives. I am absolutely grateful for their gifts, which are now here for you to read, discover, and learn from. Dr Sarah Brown, Geoffrey Berwind, Debra Englander, Raia King, for believing in me as an Author, a Storyteller, for your kind words of encouragement and for generously sharing your knowledge and wisdom. Many blessings to you all.

ONE

The Miracle of Life:
"Remember to Breathe Some Fresh Air"

I have worked all my life in that factory just across the road, half a mile from my house. Every morning I woke up at the same time, five o'clock, along with my dear wife. We had a hot homemade breakfast just after biting into some fresh garlic, and then I made my way to work. We had three lovely children. They dressed themselves, and we all left the house at the same time, only they had to turn left, and I had to go straight ahead. I guess life takes many turns.

If I was working long days, my wife prepared some food for me, such as stuffed grape leaves, which was my favourite. Meat was not consumed every day, we only had it on special occasions, such as on Easter, when a roast lamb would be consumed by the whole family.

At the factory, we made cement, so it got quite dusty in there. We ground raw materials, including limestone and clay, to a fine powder and then that was heated to the remarkably high temperature of 1450 degrees Celsius. The downside of that is that we were not wearing any protective equipment.

Then I started coughing, the cough just would not go away. I went to see my doctor with my wife, and he advised me to take a holiday in the mountain to have some fresh air. That is how we built a house there. I have so many fond memories of us running around in the field, picking up herbs that were meticulously added to our meals. Our children played constantly. I was getting better and better.

Around us at the height of the mountains, we saw numerous fields filled with dandelions. All our friends and relatives could be seen collecting them, because they knew how good this flower was and how to prepare it and make it into a delicious dish. As they were bitter if eaten raw, they had to be boiled and served with lemon and fresh olive oil. They are such a perfect side dish in Greece!

My advice for you, children and grandchildren, is to remember to breathe some fresh air. Go to the countryside, to the sea, to the mountain. We take nature for granted, we owe her, not the other way around. A newborn baby takes his first breath in this world, grows, becomes an adult. We naturally age, and we remember how much air, clean air, is crucial for our well-being.

—Dimitris K.

TWO

Imagine, You Create:
"Have a Go at It,
You Are More Able than You Think"

I remember clearly how I used to play constantly with my younger sister Pamela, who was always smiling and happy. We had our special games we used to play with other children in the village. Our favourites were Chhupam Chhupai, known here as hide and seek, and stapoo, known as hopscotch.

We always came back home, chuckling and completely dirty. I did not mind at all getting a little dirty while playing. Pameela, on the other hand, did not enjoy that part at all. I would chase her around with my hands full of mud and give her a gentle squeeze, she then ran towards home screaming, and only calmed down once she plunged herself in a bucket filled with clean water. I was so mischievous, but in a nice way, I loved my sister to bits, but I could not resist this exquisite temptation!

As the years passed, I turned into a young woman. I knew how to cook, sew clothes, and look after my loved ones. I was ready to be married and have children of my own. I met my husband and we moved to London, as he was working for an international information technology company.

Everything was different, and I had to adjust to the new life and make some new friends. That was undeniably difficult at first. I gradually got accustomed to the new way of life. I called my family every week, remembering the time zone difference, as I didn't want to wake them up at night.

I had my two boys one year apart, and they were now nine and ten.

My children became fervent admirers of electronic games. They came home talking about a different game each day, and I could not follow what they were talking about. I encouraged them to create their own toys and games, and I always had some art and craft resources available at home. One afternoon, we all sat at the table in the garden, and my sons came up with some characters. Vanish was quite good at drawing, so he sketched, and with his brother's and my help we created a model. We tried different ways; it was not always a success, but we always had loads of fun.

We also came up with an idea: one game bought for one game made. I have a lovely collection of all their creations. They are all unique, they have learnt so much by making them through trial and error, which was definitely part of the process.

Dear children and grandchildren, have a go at it. You are more able than what you think. Create, create, create! The rewards are endless and the process invaluable!

—Shanti P.

THREE

Growing Up:
"Know Who You Are,
It Does Not Matter Where You Come From"

It was fifty years ago, and I was only thirteen. A big change was about to happen in my life.

I grew up in a small village near the blue mountain in Jamaica. I woke up every morning, glancing at the beautiful mist coming out from its heights. For breakfast, I had a banana, an orange, and a cup of tea. My parents owned a few farm holdings. My father was also a builder and a policeman, and my mum was also leading a busy life, as she looked after the farm, the family, and our home. My parents employed people to help with the farm, pick the crops, and take them to the market downtown.

Our mother instilled an entrepreneurship mindset early on in our life.

Growing up in a large family with six siblings and watching my parents managing everything around us so effectively has had an effect on us. All of the skills my parents developed and mastered in front of our eyes were transferred to us naturally. We were also involved; we were hands on. We were not only observers, we also helped around the house too.

Mother was very keen on education, so we grew up with great values. Honesty was paramount. Every day, I got ready for school, ate a banana, an orange, and some toast for breakfast while planning my day ahead, which included some bird hunting, trying to catch blue teats, robins, or hummingbirds,. They were so colourful, so attractive to my eyes, and to my ears, their melodious tweets were enchanting. I thrived in nature. I didn't realise how lucky we were then, as our freedom allowed us to connect with nature. I was so happy. I regularly wandered on my own, walking in the fields, finding paths through trees, just enjoying nature.

My school was two villages away, and it took about three to five miles to get there. We passed a lot of fruit on the way there, and I would pick up juicy mangoes and oranges. School was fun! We were hurrying, as we did not want to be reprimanded by our teacher for being late. That was absolutely a no-no. My school was academic, we were not taught life skills. Those were taught in a technical college.

I was one of those quiet children, a tomboy, as most of my friends were boys. I used to climb trees. When we were on the playing field that was at the bottom of the school, I played all the games, including cricket and rounders—which is quite like baseball; and I loved athletics, like high jumps. I was also a fast runner! After school, we went for a swim in the river, which was a wild thing to do. I was fearless and extremely independent. How liberating, empowering, that I was embracing God's given beauty, what an amazing natural world we live in. Who needed a swimming pool when you had a river?

I went to church quite a lot. We listened to Christian music, sang songs, and read some poetry out loud. Poetry is important for us, as words are important.

When I turned twelve years old, since I was a good pupil at school and achieved good grades, I was offered a scholarship. This opened doors to top schools in the area and offered great choices of career path.

But things were about to change. My dad left Jamaica to go to London for work, and my family joined him there, less than a year later.

I got quite upset with my parents, as I did not want to leave my friends, my school, and my life. I was not prepared for the unknown. I was a pre-teenager, and it was already a difficult time for me. This just added to the stress.

Once we started our new life in London, I missed my daily swim in the river with my friends, walking to school together, playing games, and having lunch together.

Here I did not feel free. My parents were very protective, as we were in a different country in a busy city, so we did not go out much. It was frustrating. I had to get used to the school system very quickly, as I had to fit in. I joined a mainstream secondary school. It was a girl's school.

Even though the educational system was supposedly similar, I realised that it was, in fact, quite different.

Making new friends was not that difficult, as there were a few of us from the Caribbean in my class.

What helped tremendously was listening to my dad's storytelling in the evenings. That is what made me survive: a lot of laughter at home, the best medicine of all. Dad was quite an entertainer, and he really kept us going. I still feel a bit … inside. I go back to Jamaica once a year, as I still have some family there. I see everything with a different eye, but it feels warm inside and my memories start flooding. I instantly feel reinvigorated when I am there. It is such a good feeling! When I go back to Jamaica, I find my true self again, a child at heart who embarked on a life-journey but did not forget her roots.

My message to you, children and grandchildren is to know who you are, it does not matter where you come from. Know your roots, know something about your history. It is important for you and your children.

—Veronica K.

FOUR

Run and Score:
"Look after Yourself,
Really Nurture Yourself
and Your Wants."

I was living on a farm just outside a small village named Kelamata in Greece. We were making our own olive oil and our own wine. This was the pride of our family, the result of our hard work and sweat, but also the life essence, fuel which would be passed on from generation to generation.

We acquired a good work ethic, as everything would get done, including looking after the animals and cooking. Whether it was raining, snowing, or windy, we made sure that all of the chores were completed. This taught us to accept that certain things were out of control, and we just adapted to the situation.

I am so grateful to have led such a simple life, but again filled with happiness and some sadness, too.

Growing up, I loved reading. I just disappeared for hours on end, either inside the barn or somewhere in the field. I was devouring every book that landed on my lap, but my favourite ones were the ones about religion. I also enjoyed reading various magazines and I was very keen on quiz puzzles.

I just loved learning; it kept my spirit alive all those years. I have one regret, though. I wanted to go to university to learn more, but my parents never agreed with it. Later in life, once I got married and had my own children, I was struck by a tragedy, which took me many years to heal from. I was leading a very normal life, working at the farm and raising my children. My children were my pride. Then one morning, we received a phone call from the local police. My heart stopped its count. I was breathing heavily, my eyes started getting teary.

My son had an accident. He did not make it; he did not survive. At that instant, my whole world collapsed on itself.

He was only twenty years old. He had many dreams he wanted to accomplish, but was given no time to fulfil them. He was gone too early, too young.

I prayed a lot. I did not want to victimize myself; I was not a victim.

I went through a period of bereavement, different emotions were firing in me, first a total silence, subsequently followed by a denial, anger, depression, and I finally accepted it and started healing. I gave myself some time.

The whole family was a great support. We shared dear memories of him with my husband, and we frequently visited his grave, keeping it clean, and arranging some new flowers each time.

At times, to numb the pain my husband had more wine than usual.

Working at the farm, being with the animals and close to nature was gradually easing my pain. I started looking at the future again, with new promises, new hopes. My family was there. Our love for each other and our deep belief in God in Life kept us together.

My advice to you, children and grandchildren, is first to look after yourself, really nurture yourself. Your wants, your needs must be acknowledged and acted upon. Do not wait. Act now, and make choices for yourself, as you know the best what makes you happy.

—Georgia K.

FIVE

My First Trip:
"Keep Your Dreams Alive,
Don't Lose Track of Them"

I was so innocent and worriless as I grew up in the village of Ghardimou, outside the capital of Tunisia.

I was raised in a farm along with my brothers and sisters. I was running freely in the surrounding lands.

My older brother was going to school, and I wondered why I was not allowed to go with him. I, too, wanted a school bag, a school uniform. I relentlessly wondered why I was not given the opportunity to learn.

I had my own aspirations. I wanted to travel, to go to Europe.

Sitting on a big, hard rock, under an unyielding hot sun, I was selecting the green beans and trimming off the tough ends as instructed by my loving mother.

She was working so hard, and I wanted to help her. She did all of the cooking, washing, and catering for our animals.

I remember how tasty those prickly pears were, and how many times I stung my fingers trying to peel them. My mother's food was the best. We ate couscous, a dish made of steamed semolina, served with vegetables and meat—chicken, beef, or mutton, and sometimes with fish.

My mother also made *shakshouka*, *tajine*. Our relatives sometimes invited us, and we would have a *mechoui*, a traditional North African roast. It was such a nice, warm atmosphere.

My weakness was sugar. In the night, I would wake up, sneak to our kitchen, take a handful of white sugar, and put it in my mouth. It tasted so sweet, but now my teeth are no longer here, and I must watch my sugar intake.

Our soukh was so busy that everyone had a list of things to buy. I always stayed close to my mum so as to not get lost in the crowd. The selection of fruits and vegetables was staggering, and the beautiful smells of spices tickled my nostrils and I sneezed continuously. But they tasted so delicious.

We lived far from the sea, and I promised myself that one day I would go there. Days were passing by, I was growing up, and I could not wait to find my first paid job.

My dad passed away when I was young, so I do not remember him that well, I just know that he loved us all dearly.

The day of my emancipation finally arrived. A lady in town needed a housekeeper, and I was in my late teens by then. My brother accompanied me to their house. I had a small suitcase with a few things in it, a few clothes and my hairbrush, as I had to keep my long hair nice and tidy.

I had mixed emotions. I was excited, but at the same time worried, and I felt a knot in my stomach when my new employer opened the door. A mid aged lady of a short height looked at me, scrutinizing each detail of my person. I really felt awkward, and wondered if it was a good idea to be there. My brother probably felt my discomfort, and stood by my side. He started the conversation, introducing me. Then things started to ease. We were invited into the house, and offered some mint tea with some sweets. The lady told us that both she and her husband were both busy. She was a midwife and her husband was an accountant. She needed help with the house cleaning and cooking, and they had no children of their own.

I gradually grew in confidence and quickly learnt the duties. I was young and very active, and I was doing absolutely everything—house-cleaning, cooking, and laundry. The couple took me with them to the seaside on their off days, as they really cared for me.

There was one scary incident when I returned from the dentist. I had one of my teeth extracted, and as soon as I reached their house, blood started gushing everywhere, and I could feel myself passing out. They quickly called the doctor. I was told to rest for two weeks, and they cared for me as their own daughter.

In the spring, Anabella was busy getting everything ready, as she and Paulo were planning to go to Italy on holiday. I was ecstatic, as they told me they would take me with them.

It would be the first time I go on the plane and visit Europe!! *My first trip*, I thought.

Two weeks before the trip, Anabella recruited another lady, younger than me, with very strong arms, and she was assigned to do the laundry. It felt strange having her with us, as she was both overpowering and mousy. One day I was having lunch with her in the kitchen, while Anabella and Paulo were dining together in the living room.

Then Anabella called me, as she needed more bread. We were all having some delicious spaghetti cooked by her own hands. When I returned to the kitchen, half of my dinner was gone and I could see

Malika munching on it. I didn't say anything, as I didn't want any arguments. So, I became very wary of her.

As we were nearing the day of the trip, Anabella called me in, and said, "Malika will travel with us to Italy. We need her to do the laundry. We will be away for three weeks, so you can spend some time with your family, and we will see you when we are back." My heart was crushed in that instant. I could not believe what I was hearing.

The next day, I decided that I would not return and work for them. *I will find another job*, I told myself.

On their return from Italy, they came all the way to my parents' house to convince me to go back with them, but I didn't.

I promised myself that the first trip abroad, which I knew would happen sooner rather than later, would be on my terms. As it happened, that was my trip to France!

Children, grandchildren, keep your dreams alive. Don't lose track of them. Make them happen, the power is in your hands with the help of God.

—Haoua H.

SIX

My Wedding:
"Collect Many Memories of Your Childhood,
They Are Priceless"

I was a village girl, born and grew up in Aduni, a very remote place out of Hyderabad. I was not tall at all, my friends would all exceed me in height, but I was active and would always be found playing in the water. I loved how my mum brushed my hair at night, applying some coconut oil. It would instantly be embellished, feel smooth to the touch, and smell beautifully. This is a beauty ritual that I have always kept. My mother was kind-hearted and hardworking. She married young, a tradition that I would also honour myself.

My hair to this day is shiny and healthy. I hardly have any white hair, and this at the age of fifty-seven.

My father passed away when I was three years old, so I do not remember him that well. He was known to be a strong man; my mum was always telling me stories about him. There was a huge stone that was right in the middle of the village. He was the only man who could lift it easily. That event generated much envy and jealousy around him. Unlike many men who aged gracefully and left behind happy memories, he had a sudden death.

The day he died, nobody knew what had happened. Some believed he had been poisoned. Everything went so fast. I only remember the cries, and images of the burial are still anchored in my memory.

Many years later, I woke up to a beautiful day, the monsoon had just started. Some gorgeous smells made my stomach gurgle even more, and I opened my eyes wide and searched for my mother. She was standing by the door and was kindly looking at me, holding some delicious *chappati* in her hand. I quickly came out of my bed, which consisted of beautiful, handcrafted mats. In the colder months, a carpet below the mat kept us warm.

I helped my mum to lay out the breakfast. We had rotis dosas— which are crepes made of lentils, or idlis—steamed rice-dough pancakes, and different dips and chutneys as well as spiced potatoes. I was so grateful for the food we had, and religiously thanked god.

That day started as usual, I was running around with my friends, I was not going to school. At a distance, I could see men and women from our village farming rice.

The labour was excruciating, hours and hours of hard work. Rice plants took 120 days to grow from seeds to mature plants. Farmers had to flood the rice fields, because rice has better growth and produces higher yields when grown in flooded soils. When I returned home, two men—tall and charismatic—were standing in front of my house. I had never seen them before. The older one was talking to my uncle, and then they shook hands. I was standing behind a tree, so I was out of sight and decided to wait a little longer before returning home, as I felt quite uncomfortable and wary. I was only fourteen years old.

The next day, two men with now-familiar faces came to my house. I was then formally introduced to my future husband. A young sixteen-year-old boy was standing in front of me. *He was good looking,* I thought.

Later, people wondered how I managed to marry such a handsome boy.

The day of the wedding, there was a police investigation as I was only fourteen years old. My soon-to-be father-in-law had to explain himself, and he told the police that they had to go to eight villages to find a wife for his son, and that no father would give their daughter away as they didn't trust anyone coming from the city, Mumbai, where his whole family had settled in.

He reassured the police by telling them that I would stay with my family until the age of sixteen and then move to Mumbai to live with my future husband and his family.

The day of the wedding started to unravel itself quite unrealistically. I knew I was to be married, but I didn't quite process it. It was all a blur.

As a tradition, newlyweds sit on a cow carriage that takes them around the village. As I was noticeably short, some women started piling up pillows for me to sit on, as it was important that my husband and I appear to be of the same height. To lure the indiscreet even further, I was surrounded by many people from the same village, most of us were related. Everyone had an important job to do, some helped with the food, some women looked after me, arranging my hair and my sari. The drummers started playing, leading us towards the church. The church could not contain everyone, and some were standing by the entrance while others were either standing or sitting inside.

My sari was beautifully ornamented, glistening white colour with golden thread, and matching natural flowers had been arranged in my hair, which was up in a bun. The priest started the ceremony. I was listening to his words attentively and was standing there solemnly next to my husband to be. After the Father's blessing, John put a tali around my neck, a necklace made with white flowers. In my turn, I symbolically placed one around his neck. A new life was about to start for me. I was stepping up into adulthood, I felt all the love around me and as I turned around, and I could see the pride in my uncle's eyes and so much love and tenderness in my mum's. I was overwhelmed with emotion, but happy.

My advice to you, children and grandchildren, collect many memories of your childhood, they are priceless. As time goes by, they move further and further away as you build a new life for yourself. I remember tenderly all those playful times where I would not worry, but let my imagination run loose. They make me smile to this day.

—Pamela Madri

SEVEN

The Land of Hopes:
"Be Free to Be Who You Want to Be"

As my stomach gurgled, I was selling some peanuts at the market, watching people walking by. I was barefoot, and my clothes were torn. My heart was even more hurt. I had lost my mother when I was young. She was soon replaced by a stepmom who had a heart of stone. She sent me in the early morning to get her some fruits and vegetables from town. On my return, I would be welcomed with a stick and a long, cold glance. My father didn't help. He either ignored me or afflicted me with the same treatment.

I had two choices: Either stay in this life of misery and mistreatment or run for my life. That's exactly what I did when I was only eleven years old. I started by begging, then I went on cleaning people's shoes on the street, then I was selling peanuts, singing along with the song of a beggar.

Some days I ate and some days I had to go without. Each night, I found a street corner to sleep, but I had to stay vigilant, as there were criminals around. I grew up this way, alone, but I had some hope. I wanted to learn and to travel. I was not defeated. It would be a long way, but I would go step by step. I had to grow up fast and learn new skills.

Despite of my sad start in life, I was hungry; hungry for life, hungry for success. I had dreams. I had to find a way, my way. When I turned sixteen, I wanted to join the French Army, but I was told I was too young, I had to wait two more years.

I went to war in Indochina. I survived it, not only physically but mentally. I have so many stories to recount. One night, more than three hundred soldiers were in camp sleeping. I was in my bed when I heard the screams and the sounds of machetes through the night. I only had the time to slide under my bed, and the enemy was in our tent. Almost everyone in the camp was killed that night, only fifteen soldiers survived, and I was one of them.

When I returned to Tunisia, I bought two houses with the money I saved. I was thinking of the future, my future. I wanted to have a family, children. I got married young, at nineteen years old, but my mother-in-law did everything she could to separate me from my wife. She had views on a rich man for her daughter.

We had a daughter, and they tried to stop me from seeing her, so I tried to run away with my daughter, but they stopped us.

I hadn't fulfilled my wish yet, and I decided to remarry, this time in France. My work colleague introduced me to his sister. We have five beautiful daughters together. I am very proud of each one of them, and I love them dearly. I provided them with everything I was denied when I was a little boy: love, shelter, food, education, inspiration, and motivation. I wanted them to be strong, independent, and to have choices in life. I encouraged them to write: letters, assignments, anything, but master the skills of writing. I provided opportunities to enhance and support their education. Since I was not wealthy, I could not afford to pay private tuition for them. One lady, who was retired went to the Club Hippique where I was working to do horseback riding. She used to be an English teacher. One of my daughters loved languages, so naturally I connected them to one another. There was another lady, who was also retired, she was a French teacher and offered to teach my children during the school holidays. Where there is a will, there is a way.

If my children failed an exam, I encouraged them to keep going, to try again until they succeeded. I said, "No matter how many times you try, you get better at it each time until you achieve your goal."

My advice to you, children and grandchildren, be free to be who you want to be. You can be anything you want. Life is an oyster, and you are a jewel.

—Ahmed M

EIGHT

My Regrowth:
"Drink in Moderation,
Don't Deny if You Have a Problem"

I remember my early years. At the tender age of seventeen I had my first drink, but not my last.

Every night I would dread the next morning. I was helpless; drinking was an uncontrollable need. I had to have it. In the early morning, I woke up in sweat and my lovely hands were shaky. I didn't recognize them, and I didn't recognize myself. I had always been in control of myself, my life, and now I was losing the grasp of it.

I was grasping for air, I needed my everything, my drink. As I was getting ready for work, I also made sure to pack an extra support in my bag.

At work, I always found an excuse to go to the toilet, disappear in the corridor, and find myself standing in front of my locker.

From there, I carefully hid the bottle under my blouse. I shivered at the thought of being found. The only safe place to have it was the toilet. This was the beginning of my downfall.

No one was fooled, as my mint sweets were not enough to hide the smell. Everyone remained silent, turning a blind eye to the problem, to my problem. I had no one to talk to there, everyone was just busy making an income and that was about it. I felt very lonely.

I was a chef by trade, and I loved my job. I worked for Nestle for about four years. One day I had to face it: I had a problem and I had to deal with it. I went to my doctor, and they sent me to the local hospital for two weeks to detox. That was tough, but I was determined. I had to take myself out of my familiar environment where my destructive habits started. For me to be cleared of alcohol, I made a difficult decision to save my life, but I was also heartbroken, as I had to leave my family behind at least for a while. But for how long?

Then I started the process. I had to get funded by the NHS, as the treatment would be onerous. That was not easy, as I had to show that I was a heavy drinker and had become addicted to alcohol. According to them, I was not drinking enough. I had to show and convince them I needed help, and the worry led to many sleepless nights.

I kept having this phrase in my head: "One is too many and one thousand is not enough." I had to go through three stages for my recovery and three different rehabs. It took me six years.

The first rehab I went to is the one I remember very well; we were in a big house with eleven rooms. Our days were tightly regimented. We had a rota to follow, everyone had a job to do. No one knew how to cook, so I put myself forward.

I took my job very seriously and introduced all the health and safety procedures in the kitchen. Some laughed at it and thought that was just too much, but I took pride in implementing those measures.

It was a mixed rehab, so we had to make sure we were all dressed and ready before going down to the communal rooms. Our weekly routines were tempered with group meetings, and therapies that included acupuncture. People in the house had all sorts of problems related to addiction, some had drug overdoses and were sent there as a last resort.

Weekends were wild. The supervisors were all off, and we were left to our own devices! That meant drinks were circulating freely, and even though they got really close to me, I never gave up. I didn't want to let myself down, I had my life to go back to, my family, my children. This place was just an interlude.

Then after they all enjoyed the vodka, a glimpse of consciousness came back to them, reality hit the roof, and the testing day would irrefutably come. They didn't know what to do, then a couple of them turned to me, helpless, and asked if I could just help them with some of my urine to cover up their mischief.

At the group meetings, there was this guy, Dave, and he always ended up sitting next to me, no matter what. He had this thing, he was always picking up his toenails, that would just make my stomach twirl on itself, there was absolutely no way he would go to the kitchen and cook for me or anyone. He had to stay away from the kitchen duty.

Everyone there were heavy drinkers, most of them were hooked on spirits and a few either on beer, wine, or both.

In 2006, after staying clear of alcohol for six years, I relapsed. I didn't go to any kind of celebrations for such a long time. I promised myself to stay away from alcohol, or maybe just have one if I couldn't escape it.

I was invited to a barbecue, where I had one glass of wine, then another, and then I stopped. When I got home, I was proud of myself.

The next day, I woke up and I had this urge. I went to the shop, bought a few bottles of wine without thinking, just operating like an erratic robot. I locked myself at home and I started indulging on the wine, glasses were flying, bottles were emptying. That was not enough, that was never enough, I had to have more. I substituted water with alcohol. My partner, who was also a heavy drinker, was joining in the decadence. I got to the point where I started regularly drinking up to twelve bottles of wine every day. This downfall lasted about a year.

I had another wake-up call, a last chance for survival. I knew exactly what to do, I had been there before. I called my GP, went on a detox for two weeks, and then on to rehab.

* * *

Later on, I learnt that I had an addictive personality. Now, thirteen years later, I am thankfully clear of alcohol. I had to sacrifice a few things along the way, including my marriage, which was toxic. The change of environment was my saviour.

I am fifty-nine years old, and I consider myself a survivor. I celebrated my son's wedding in America last year. That was amazing and unforgettable. He organized the trip for me. He made me feel so special, so loved.

As I was recovering, I wanted to be a counsellor for addiction. I went to study at Lewisham College and in the middle of it I stopped. My wounds were still there and would not allow me to go any further.

My dear readers, my experience has been tough, but I have learnt from it. I have grown into this older version of myself, physically diminished with various ailments I have collected along the way.

My advice to you is drink in moderation, don't deny if you have a problem. If you have a problem do not leave it, damages cannot be rectified.

Out of three people, one makes it, one dies, and one keeps going back and forth. Today I am alive to tell you my story and speak the truth.

—Pat P

NINE

Changes:
"Believe in Yourself!
Go and Venture the World"

Not good enough to do anything, but why? In my forties, I was going to defy my wrongly instilled self-beliefs. I went back to nursing school! That did not come easy at all, I had to work hard at my math. It was a long and tedious journey, but I was determined. Enough was enough, I had to stand for myself, for my life choices. I would thrive and be happy, truly happy.

While my husband supported me overall, he did not like the timing and wanted me to wait until he had finished his studies. My children did not like the idea too much either, since much of my time would be occupied studying, but I knew my time was now and I had the overwhelming feeling that if I would not do it now, I would maybe lose the courage to do it at all.

The road that led me back to self-empowerment was through listening to podcast sessions focusing on my personal growth.

I drew my inspiration from a multitude of teachers, some published and some not. I studied psychology in high school. I gradually emancipated myself, my next career was to be a travel nurse, and both my husband and I followed the same career path. This was not the ultimate destination, but a means to it.

I only spent eight grades in the United States before moving back to Germany. I grew up in Germany and met my husband there. We met at work, working for the U.S. Army. In 1995, we moved back to New York near the Canadian border and later, in 1997, to West Virginia where we have lived since.

Since then, I have only gone back to Germany once, in 2003. Growing up, I remember my mum always cooking, those delicious smells embalmed the house, food was a delicatessen, traditional sauerbraten, roast beef stew, potato dumplings and pancakes. Ah, I missed fine cheese and meat so much ... I missed all of it! My mum loved to entertain and feed people with her love of food, which is why I believe I overeat today. I grew up in the city, but I always lived within walking distance to water, which I feel a natural connection and attraction to. In Germany it was the Rhine River, and in West Virginia I live near a lake.

I grew up very close to natural beauty, which I am very fond of to this day. I get reinvigorated every time I go out for a stroll to the park by the lake.

I made friends for life in Germany, and I have also learned to be bilingual. From 1995 to 2003 I did not go back there, and it was such a long, long time.

My first job was in medical coding. I had a three-month contract, then I moved to Massachusetts and got another job there for seven months.

There were loads of politics in my workplace. Why would people thrive in troubles? That just did not make any sense to me.

Everywhere I worked, I learnt some new skills. The first month was very stressful and intense, as there was not enough permanent staff. As I was heading back home after my long and eventful night shift, I just told myself, *Quality of life, maybe one day, in Portugal!*

I wanted money, independence, and to achieve financial freedom. I just went for a career change at the age of forty-seven.

I was lucky, though, that the place we lived in was close to a natural park. It was such a blessing to wake up each morning to that beautiful sight. In my previous position, the hospital had one hundred and eighty-two beds in rural Nebraska with a mixed eighteen-bed psychiatric floor where patients of all ages were admitted. The youngest one we took care of was nine years old. We treated a range of psychiatric illness from eating disorders and drug addiction to psychosis/mania and, of course, depression. Most nights, my shift ran from six p.m. till six a.m., and it was just me working with a female mental health specialist. Psychiatrists were on call, sometimes in other states, and I was responsible for pre-screening admissions.

It is stressful not knowing where and with whom you will work on any given shift and what mood the patients may be in that particular night. In general, when you work in psych you have to have a thick skin, as you will be insulted on a regular basis. I have been body slammed, hit, spit at, and stabbed with pen, and had various fluids thrown at me, I could go on. You will be challenged, and you have to remain calm. Working in a psychiatric environment is challenging, and I learnt to stand for myself.

The best part is when you know you have made a difference for one person. It doesn't happen as often as I would like, but when it does it is priceless.

My plan is to live about thirty minutes outside of a medium-sized city in a moderate climate in a self- sufficient house with enough land for small-scale farming, and maybe just work two days a week for the health insurance, not sure where, in the States. My second choice is to move to Portugal. I am a permanent traveller, as I have grown to love the unknown. Or is it how I was all along?

My advice to you, children, grandchildren, is to believe in yourself! Go and venture the world. Time is limitless, growth is endless, reach for the stars, be who you want to be, help yourself! Speak for yourself, set limits.

Learn how to follow your intuition, as it will never fail you. It always works out at the end. Someone is looking after me, after you. I met good people, at the right time.

—Dagmar H

TEN

A New Dawn, a New Me:
"Stop and Rewind,
Take the Time to Find Yourself"

I woke up drenched in sweat. I finally realised something that would change the rest of my life: I deserved better!

My self-esteem had been crushed, my personality had cracks. I only saw myself in pieces, an eggshell endlessly, terminally bruised. I had to pick up the pieces for my own sanity, for me, but how?

I did not know where to start. I was so confused, so damaged inside, that every morning I would wake up, shaken. Memories, ah memories, where have you gone? Those images are blurred, I cannot remember, I do not want to remember. It is so painful!

There is a place, my birthplace, which could be a good start. I was born and grew up in the Philippines. I was sheltered and raised by Ya-Yas, also known as nannies. When my father was out of the country to attend important duties, the Ya-Yas ruled the roost.

I would not even dream of disobeying. The country was very superstitious, and strict discipline was instilled to keep us on a straight line. I was an incredibly quiet child. I grew up close to my brother, my mother had left the house when I was one year old. She was not part of our daily routine. I grew up without a mother. I had only known a life of inconstancy. I later met her when I was six years old, and again when I was fourteen.

My house was filled with rare ornaments, ranging from precious paintings to exquisite vases and furniture. Growing up, I was also surrounded by all of those beautiful women. My dad dated many different women, all at once. He taught us to keep secrets about them. Dad said, "If any of these women find out about each other because of you, you will each get a spanking!"

One of those women who Dad dated was my ballet teacher. She had short, natural red hair, and long legs. She came to me and said, "I am going to teach you ballet." I was only six years old then. I was not immediately thrilled by it, as I was torn with anguish at the idea of failing and disappointing my father. I learnt later that she was the director of the Miss Philippines Beauty Pageant and beloved by all.

My father had instructed her to deliver some lessons to me. I don't remember it being an urge I had to fulfil, it was just another lesson I had to attend, but gradually a passion grew in me.

Evenings were always filled with loads of background noises. There were parties after parties, an incessant tumult, echoing the heavy showers that were so familiar, and typhoons were also common natural disasters. The maids, my brother, and I showered outside in the open! The warm water washed away the soap from our hair.

At night, we could hear frogs, crickets, cockroaches, and beetles. The Ya-Yas would take a thread and attach it around a flying beetle's legs. We would hold on to the thread like they were balloons with wings.

In the mornings, I would drink fresh coconut juice. I watched as the chauffeurs climbed up the trees barefoot to hack down those coconuts with a huge bolo knife. The chef cooked some traditional food for my brother and me: chicken adobo, lumpia, pancit bihon, or dinuguan. On hot days, we had a tasty and refreshing halo-halo.

Early in the morning, I waited for the chauffeur to take me to school. I went to a Catholic school. Days there were long and laborious. On the way there, I could see workers and pupils travelling in the local bus, the jeepney, which was so colourful and unique, as each one was decorated differently. It was so fun to watch, I thought.

As I was nearing school, I remembered stories my dad told me about my great- grandfather, Thomas Henry Edwards. He was a white Spaniard and the first man to come to teach English in The Philippines in 1910. He passed away at the age of seventy-six years old and was the last Thomasite.

During the school holiday, we went to Bagulo and stayed in our holiday home. I have so many good memories there. It was up in the mountains; the weather was cold and frosty. It was such a relief from the heat and humidity in Manila. I would do my favourite activity, horseback riding.

At nine years old, I moved to the United States At thirty -five, I started a career in the entertainment industry, working as a dancer.

I went on to try to find an agent, which was a big struggle, then at the age of thirty-seven I worked on a cruise ship as a magician's assistant. I went on to become one of the leaders and, through hard work and determination, I became a manager a few years later. Learning to dance is easier than teaching dance, and I did not know how to teach dance. Teaching requires one to have authority, and I was underdeveloped when it came to telling people what to do, so I improvised and assigned the stronger dancers to teach.

Throughout my career I was constantly reminded of my age and told, "You are too old, try something else."

But I had to believe in myself. I was not worthless, but I was not well equipped as a child to recover from past emotional traumas. I had to rebuild myself and find some tools in the form of personal development programs. I had little money to my name, and I had limited beliefs.

The journey to find myself took twenty years. I signed on to some programs, I meditated, and I learnt about myself, my needs, and my wants. If you don't like how your life is going, then you can create something totally different, you will get the life that you create.

My advice to you: Do not settle for less, there are so many programs and coaches, it is your responsibility to be happy. Take back ownership of your own happiness.

My advice to you children, grandchildren, is stop and rewind. Take the time to find yourself, to reconnect with who you truly are.

—Pamela M

ELEVEN

A Love Reality:
"Never Give up on Your Aspirations,
Your Desires!"

Those familiar words were resonating in my head. "This sport is not for women; you are not built for it. As I walked past the glowing white building for the tenth time, I decided that today was going to be different. It was a life-changing moment.

I had an inner call; I had to listen to the call of my soul. I profoundly needed to be me, myself, regardless of what people would say or think.

Taekwondo, an ancestral martial art, resonated perfectly well with me. No matter how hard I would have to train for it, I wanted to challenge myself, to get the best from myself!

I did not need to prove anything to anyone, I was doing this for myself. As I kept walking down the street, my heart was pumping, my eyes started blurring, my hands trembled. All of my movements were in discord, I was such an inharmonious musical instrument.

Taekwondo, Tae Kwon Do, or Taekwondo, a Korean martial art, characterized by its emphasis on head-height kicks and fast kicking techniques like Tang Soo Do.

I was only in my twenties when I started taking Taekwondo classes. There were different movement to remember, forms, and techniques. It could all be overwhelming, but I kept practising again and again until I got it all right. I was a fast learner, and totally committed to the art.

There was an issue, though, at the training centre: the behaviour of our Master was totally inappropriate towards girls. He had to be challenged. A few other members of the club decided to join me, only I was let down at the crucial moment. One other member and I channelled all of the possible courage we found within ourselves to go and see the Den. On that evening when I got home, the unexpected happened, and I received a letter of acceptance to another Taekwondo centre. That was a miracle!

Sometime after that, I completed coaching training and became a coach myself! It was nice to be on the other side for a change! I also wanted to try some Karate, so I had a go at it, but that was not for me.

Then it all stopped. I got married and was on a new wave of my life. With the support of my husband, I retrained. What a great motivator!

One day I took my grandchild to his Taekwondo competition, which brought back a thirst in me. I was ready to re-embark on the wagon. The love of martial arts is exceptional, but this time around I wanted a more traditional form of Taekwondo, so I started searching for it!

Who said things you love are only a step away? Well, my new Taekwondo centre happened to be only two minutes away from home.

As I started re-training, I could hear people around me mumbling, "Look, she is starting this sport now ... isn't she too old for it?"

I was ignoring those disgraceful comments. Instead I just kept telling myself, *Come on, keep going, you can do this.* I was pushing myself.

Until one day I woke to beautiful sunlight caressing my forehead. As I was stretching my arms, a tiger raw came out of me. I was ready!

I got up, made myself a healthy breakfast, got ready, and made my way to the Taekwondo centre. I entered the building. Many people were gathering on the benches, I inhaled deeply as I pushed open the door to the changing room.

"Miss Brenda!" My name was called, and it was my turn to compete.

I will never forget that day, the day I returned home with a black belt! And this at the age of fifty!

My message to you:

Never give up on your aspirations, your desires! There is no need to compare yourself to others. Be the best you can be, for you. Awake the grey tiger in you!

Do not be afraid to fall, but learn how to do it safely. Give yourself some love, some care, and stand up again on both feet.

—Brenda S

TWELVE

A Recipe for Happiness:
"Slow the Heartbeat,
Breathe, Enjoy Each Moment"

Today I celebrated my 100th Birthday. What a beautiful life I have had!

My house was perched high in the mountains, that is how I lived all my life.

I had my battles, many years ago when I fought in the second world war.

I am from Volos. I never wanted to settle in Athens, as I like calm and peacefulness. Nature provides me with everything I need, and it is stress free!

No need to go to the supermarket, I grow everything I need. I have also grown to know the names and properties of many plants in my area. I was a self-made botanist, making concoction for all my ailments.

I made my very own nettle tea! I stayed as far as possible from doctors; I did not need them!

I loved the fresh evenings, the smell of cypress, softly brushed by the summer breeze. What a delight, what an honour to be part of it.

Every day was a new day for me, I saw and learnt new things. I spent long period of times reflecting and appreciating what I had and where I was. Nothing made me worried; my motto was: "If you want to live longer, don't worry." So I did not. It was so much easier and so rewarding. My health and long life are a testament to it.

Listen to the birds, take strolls in nature, make your own food, enjoy eating your food. By taking your time, observe, learn how to be silent, and appreciate those precious moments.

My advice to you, children and grandchildren, slow the heartbeat, breathe, enjoy each moment of your life. Do not fast forward, be there, now.

—Yannis K

THIRTEEN
Healthy Life: "Keep Yourself Active"

I lived all my life in a small village in Greece. I lost my husband to illness, but I cherished our life together till his last day. We never moved away, as we did not feel the need to. I loved cooking homemade dishes, a new dish for each day with local products. I used to walk with my granddaughter to the market.

We picked the vegetables to make delicious dishes: stuffed vegetables and fish soups.

Greek salads and sourdough bread were always on the table at mealtimes.

Gorgeous smells came out of the kitchen window and anyone approaching the house was enamoured by those sublime smells, a mixture of herbs, fish, or chicken, slowly cooked in the homegrown olive oil.

Those frugal times were followed by periods of long fasting and would usually occur either before Christmas or Easter.

I was so happy to have my granddaughter with me, and I instilled in her the important things to remember in life, starting from following a rigid daily routine. Every day without fault we woke up between 5 and 6 a.m. I washed my face with clear water and olive soap and only applied some Nivea cream. I then took off my hair rollers that I rigorously applied each evening before going to bed. My hair was detangling as if the strands had a life of their own, then I shook them off before putting them back up in a bun. I wore a long skirt and a jumper of dark colours since the loss of my husband. My look was very sober.

I prepared a hot breakfast consisting of my homemade marmalade, cheese, yoghurt, bread, sour milk, and boiled eggs.

We then got ourselves ready to walk to church. I was a Christian Orthodox. Spirituality has always taken an important place in my life and in my heart, and has given me such a support in hard times, but also in good times and this since I was a little girl. After church, I spent a few hours cross stitching. I made so many beautiful and practical things with my hands: blankets, decorated pillowcases, table covers. That is a skill that I have never forgotten, I was cross-stitching until the age of ninety-six. It helped me to keep great dexterity in my hands, as I had to concentrate on my work of art, my designs.

I kept my house spotless. I did all the housecleaning, dishes, and washing my clothes. I was independent and able to do all the chores. That kept me going for many, many years.

I had a TV, but really, I just turned it on to have some background noise.

My health has always been amazing, thanks to the help of God and my family.

My advice to you, children and grandchildren, is to always keep yourself active, not by overdoing it but by primarily making rudimentary things yourself. Make your own bread, grow your own vegetables, make things with your hands, and be spiritual, pray. It helped me all my life and guided me.

—Chrysoula C

FOURTEEN

Fond Memories:
"Embrace Life, Make the Most of It"

As soon as the sun rose, I was up on both feet, ready for the day ahead. I had my vineyard to attend. It was in the early fall, and we had to check with my workers if the grapes were ripe and ready to harvest. We grew things naturally, without any pesticides.

I took one in my hand. It was rich in colour, juicy, and full-flavoured to the taste. It was quite plump to the eye, then I had to do the test of the hand. I easily crushed it.

They were ready! It took us about three years to produce viable red grapes. We always have prosperous weather in Greece and great light, and we look after our soil intensely, making sure it is well-drained. The result was there! Our production of grapes this year was really promising, and that filled me with such joy.

All of the youngsters from the village, together with my children, started picking the grapes and keeping them in baskets, ready to have the stems removed and be crushed before the primary fermentation, a process that could take up to one month.

Once yeasts converted the sugar from the grapes into alcohol, the red wine grapes were pressed, and the juice was pumped into barrels for aging. After primary fermentation, the wine was then transferred into oak barrels.

While I was in the field, my wife was cooking homemade meals: fish soups and roast dinners, as we were nearing winter. Then she looked after our farm animals. I was so grateful to have such loving, strong, and supportive wife.

Once all the work was finished, my son and I would walk back home. As we got closer to home, stars pierced the dark sky, owls flew, and foxes hunted.

We were both starving, and we were already jubilant at the thought of a hot diner.

My advice to you, children and grandchildren, embrace life, make the most of it. Do not forget to forge memories of your loved ones and of your life. These are the precious assets that you will be looking back on as you age.

—Thanasis K

Conclusion

I hope you are now inspired by all those stories and feel the need to share yours, whether an incommensurable jewel, a gift for a lifetime, a second chance, or a very first insight. Each one of us can play a part in making our world a beautiful place, inspired by our growth and ultimately our wisdom.

If you would like to share your story and leave behind a generous life testament that will benefit future generations, join Wahida on her weekly podcast: "My success, my story." Send your request via the website or send a direct email.

www.wahidamohamed.com
wahida@wahidamohamed.com

About the Author

Wahida Mohamed is interested in people's stories and the wisdom each story conveys. She is a trained secondary teacher, having gained her teaching qualifications at the Institute of Education in London, England. Her deep love of languages led her to start her own company providing language services and London-experience packages involving English classes with themed weekends around cultural events.

Her mission is to bring to light how everyone on this planet has value and wisdom to share. She continues to thrive herself through learning new things and trying things out—something she encourages the younger generation to do as well. It is her belief that this trial-and-error leads to growth.

Wahida lives in London, England, and enjoys travelling, singing, and time with friends and family.